I0214227

Copyright ©2023 Amy Baird Middleton
All rights reserved.

ISBN: 978-0-9915467-6-3

Library of Congress Control Number:
First Edition
Wren's Nest Productions LLC, Monterey, VA

The Bembo font design is an old-style humanist serif typeface originally cut by Francesco Griffo in 1495.

Baboo

and
The Queen's Garden

Amy Baird

This is a story about Baboo, a sweet young elephant who worked in the Queen's flower garden at the palace on Cloud Mountain. The garden was Baboo's favorite place in the entire kingdom.

Baboo had thoughtful, loving parents and two delightful sisters. His younger sister was called Ellie and his older sister was called Lilly. His sisters spent most of their time in the forest gathering leaves off the trees and swimming in the river.

In the early morning the sisters would roam through the tall grasses of the savannah, and in the heat of the day they would run back into the sparkling river to cool off. Ellie especially liked using her trunk as a snorkel when she was swimming in the deep part of the river.

There were often as many as fifty elephants in the herd family. They were usually kind and caring. Occasionally, some members of the herd would cause problems just like the villagers do who lived near the Palace on Cloud Mountain.

Baboo's father was a large bull elephant, and a strong father figure for the elephant herd. He guided the behavior of the young male elephants, and corrected them when they became too rambunctious.

The Queen was sitting at her desk in the Palace on Cloud Mountain writing to the heads of the villages. She was reminding them to get ready for the annual Market Day Celebration, a day for visiting with their neighbors and sharing the food they had all grown.

Sometimes the villagers took their sheep and goats to sell at the market along with hand woven wool blankets, carved wooden toys, and delicious fruit pies. Once a year they might even take a lamb, a horse or a milk cow with them to sell or trade.

The King and Queen were often occupied with the serious affairs of the kingdoms. Their little kingdom was surrounded by warring states and they had to work hard to keep their people safe and free from wars and conflict.

Luckily for the villagers, the King and his council decided that war of any kind would never be allowed in the magical kingdom. The King and his family had lived through many years of conflict and the misery it caused. They also knew that no one ever truly wins a war.

The King enjoyed playing his cello in the great hall of the Palace while he waited for his family to join him for dinner. The Queen and their daughter, Amana, would arrive before dinner in order to relax and listen to the King playing his music. Afterwards they would sit together by the warm fire and share the events of their day. Amana especially looked forward to her parents' discussions of world events and the latest news from the villages.

It was Saturday and Amana the young Princess was in the palace with her mother, the Queen, reading to her cat Sassy. When Amana put her book down she looked out the window and saw Baboo down in the garden.

Baboo had just finished his work, removing a tree that had fallen
across the path near the garden.

After Baboo completed his work for Mr. Pepper, the Queen's beloved gardener, he was often alone quietly looking at the flowers and the little bugs and birds that lived in the garden.

Amana thought it was unusual that the little elephant spent so much time in her mother's special flower garden, especially when none of the other animals in the kingdom were allowed to enter the garden.

Mr. Pepper once told Baboo that if any deer or giraffes got into the garden they would probably eat the leaves off the trees, along with the lovely flowers he had just planted for the Queen.

The Queen especially disliked the Red Billed Bubbies. She even put up a sign to keep the Bubbies out of the garden. The sign must have worked because they were only seen there once, early one morning, hurrying out of the garden. She told the princess that the Bubbies ate the precious insects, like the ladybugs, and the pink earthworms, and all the other little bugs the garden needed to keep its soil healthy in order to grow the Queen's flowers.

Baboo loved and admired the Queen. She was thoughtful and kind, and cared about all the people in her kingdom. Her people were good people, but like most people, once in a while they needed help with their problems. The Queen often talked with the villagers about their lives. She listened patiently and was usually helpful. Thankfully, most of the villagers were kind to one another and they especially understood the importance of keeping peace with their neighbors.

There were a few difficult neighbors who caused trouble in the kingdom by taking things that didn't belong to them. They might take a neighbor's hoe or wheelbarrow or even steal someone's cow. Of course, stealing a cow would be a big problem for the Queen to deal with.

The Princess enjoyed watching Baboo walk through the garden, moving his weight from side to side, as he strolled among the flowers. Baboo walked softly and never came close to stepping on the flowers, let alone the little lizards and frogs or the little pink worms that lived under the leaves and rocks.

The Princess wondered if maybe the reason Baboo was allowed to spend so much time in her mother's garden was because he never made loud noises, like the parrots and crows that lived in the trees outside of the garden.

But actually the main reason the Queen let Baboo spend time in her garden was not because he was careful not to step on her flowers or that he helped Mr. Pepper remove broken trees from the garden. The main reason the Queen allowed Baboo into her garden was because he loved and appreciated the garden's beauty and understood how much the garden meant to her. He knew the flowers gave the Queen a sense of peace and calm when she had problems to solve in the kingdom.

Sometimes Baboo would raise his trunk and sniff the fragrant garden air.

He might even use the two "fingers" on the end of his trunk to pick a
few colorful flowers, to give the Princess and the Queen.

The young elephant truly loved the flowers.

And when the Princess spent time in the garden with Baboo, she noticed that the flowers appeared to be brighter and happier when he was there. The flowers enjoyed Baboo's company, and they felt loved and appreciated by the young elephant. Baboo was so kind to them. He often told the flowers how pretty their colors were, and when their sweet fragrance filled the garden air, he said that it made him very happy.

One morning Princess Amana asked Baboo why he spent so much of his day alone in the flower garden. "After all," she said, "your herd has a beautiful forest and miles of grassland for grazing, plus a deep river for swimming. So why have you chosen to spend most of your day in my mother's flower garden."

"Well…Princess," he said, "You see, the Queen's garden has flowers that are all my favorite colors: red, blue, yellow, pink, and even bright orange, and their fragrance fills the air with a sweet scent. But more importantly, the garden is also filled with peace and quiet…and beautiful butterflies. I do love the beautiful butterflies, Princess."

"Baboo, I think I am beginning to understand the importance of a flower garden. You have helped me to appreciate my mother's garden, thank you Baboo."

"You are welcome, Princess. And by the way, you know what? The garden even has a family of songbirds. I enjoy hearing the sparkle of bird song and the serenity they bring to the garden as they fly in and out of the trees."

"If I move very slowly and softly, I can even see the butterflies floating from flower to flower. They seem to kiss each flower as they float through the garden."

"Baboo," the princess said, with a smile. "It does look like they are kissing the flowers, but they're really drinking their nectar to pollinate the flowers and the tree blossoms.
Did you know that without butterflies and bees there would be no fruit on the trees, including those bananas you love?"

The Princess was sitting by her window watching the rose-colored sunset as it filled the evening sky. She noticed Baboo's father standing by himself on the riverbank and thought he looked sad. The Princess leaned out her window and called down to Baboo to suggest that he might want to spend some time with his father. Baboo agreed with the Princess and went down to the river to be with his father.

"You look worried Papa," Baboo said. "Please tell me what you are worrying about."

"Oh Baboo," his father said sadly, "there are young male elephants in our herd who do not yet understand the ways of the herd. These adolescent elephants are rude and rambunctious, and they won't share the ball with the little elephants. They have also been disrespectful to our Matriarch, the leader of the herd.

"Most importantly," his father said, "the Matriarch teaches the young female elephants how to nurture and care for not just their own baby calves, but they must also learn to nurture and care for all the baby calves in their herd. She is the oldest female in our herd, and a very wise and beloved leader."

"Papa, you must be talking about Serena. Mother said that Serena is the most important member of the herd."

"Your mother is right, Baboo, as usual. I do admire the way your mother and Serena both guide our herd to be thoughtful, caring elephants. The reason I am sad is that the young, inexperienced males won't listen to Serena, our Matriarch, even though she is responsible for all the herd's needs. Our safety and security depends on her knowledge, and this problem is causing a great deal of unhappiness and confusion in the herd…especially to the children. Everyone is saddened by the rough behavior of the young male elephants."

Serena, the Matriarch of the herd

"And Baboo," his father said, "I am not sure I know the best way to solve this problem with these young adolescent elephants."

"Well, father," Baboo said, "the Queen also has problems like yours, but she has a flower garden where she can sit peacefully and decide the best way to solve her problems."

"Oh, I see," said his father, "but Baboo, I don't have any flowers. I don't even have a garden."

The following afternoon Baboo was standing quietly in the Queen's
flower garden trying to think of a way to help his father. The garden was peaceful and quiet, just
the hint of a warm, gentle breeze. Then just as he began feeling sleepy, the birds started singing, and
suddenly Baboo had a terrific idea!
"I know what I'll do, I will go to the Queen and discuss the problem my father is having with the
young male elephants in the herd."

The next day, after explaining the problem to the Queen, Baboo asked her where he might find flowers like the beautiful flowers in her garden. He reminded her that the flower garden had always helped the Queen solve her problems and maybe flowers could help solve his father's problems too.

"Baboo," she said softly, "I know exactly where you can find flowers. I have many flowers in my garden that I can share. Tomorrow I will ask Mr. Pepper to go down to the river and plant a garden for your father and fill it with my flowers."

Baboo was really excited that the Queen had listened to him and that she had even offered to send Mr. Pepper, her very own gardener, to plant the flowers in his father's new garden.

"The Queen is so busy," he thought, "but she took the time to listen to me and help me with my father's problem. How wonderful is that?"

"Tomorrow I will take a picnic down to the river and tell Papa my good news about his new garden."

The following day the Queen told Baboo that Mr. Pepper planned to put the flowers in his father's garden before he leaves.

"Oh, I didn't know Mr. Pepper was leaving. Where is he going?"

"He's going to Scotland," the Queen said, "to visit his brother. It's a long journey from our kingdom, but he will return before the annual Market Day Celebration. Since Mr. Pepper is a botanist I will ask him to choose the winner of the flower show on Market Day."

"I think that's a good idea," Baboo told the Queen. "We both know Mr. Pepper loves flowers.

"You know what though, I will miss him."

"I know you will," the Queen said. "By the way, just so you know, Mr. Pepper will be back here in time for your birthday."

"Oh, that's great!"

"You will soon be 10 years old Baboo," she said. "Imagine that. My little elephant is growing up."

Early the next morning Baboo filled a basket with his father's favorite foods, bananas, a variety of tree leaves and some yummy bamboo shoots. That afternoon as Baboo was putting his picnic basket down on the grass, his father hurried over to greet him.

"Guess what?" he said, "I have a surprise for you, Baboo."

"I have a new garden! In fact, Mr. Pepper just planted more flowers in my garden."

"Papa, that is what I just came here to tell you."

"Oh, thank you Baboo, for bringing a picnic. But before we eat lunch, I must remind you to thank the Queen and her gardener, Mr. Pepper, for my beautiful garden."

"I will thank both of them for you, Papa."

"I also want to thank you, Baboo, for thinking of me. Mr. Pepper told me that my flower garden was all your idea."

"Baboo, this morning while I was alone in my new garden, the answer I have been searching for finally came to me."

"I'm glad you found the answer, Papa!"

"Well," he said, "I think the answer is listening to the young male elephants with my heart and not just with my head. Baboo, I need to try harder to understand the problems of these adolescent elephants. After all, I am older and perhaps I'm wiser… at least I hope I'm wiser! I remember what it was like when I was a young male elephant, and the many difficult challenges we all face growing up."

"That must have been hard for you, Papa."

"It was hard. Now come with me, Baboo, let's go into my garden and look at those beautiful flowers. And by the way, thank you again for a delicious picnic and also for my flower garden."

"Oh, you're welcome, Papa. You know something… I hope I will always try to listen to you. You are so thoughtful and wise. I do love you, Papa."

Baboo said goodnight to his father and started up the road to the palace.

The moon and stars came out, as Baboo returned to the Queen's garden for a peaceful night's sleep.

★★ "The temple bell stops – but the sound keeps coming out of the flowers."

Basho poet 1749
Kyoto, Japan

A Little Note on the Biology of Elephant Behavior

Dear Readers of Baboo and the Queen's Garden,
I encourage everyone interested in learning more about elephants to read **Elephant Sense and Sensibility: Behavior and Cognition** *by Michael Garstang, a University of Virginia distinguished Emeritus research professor. Growing up in remote northern KwaZulu-Natal, South Africa, surrounded by diverse wildlife, embedded a lifelong engagement with animals and the natural world. Earning a doctoral degree in Meteorology and working in environmental sciences, his research ultimately led him to pioneer discoveries in elephant communication and ecosystem sustainability, as profiled in the National Geographic articles and the film "Giants of Etosha". He is also the author of Ntombazana, and other children's stories about elephants. Mr. Garstang is an experimentalist. He conducted most of his research on elephants through multiple field experiments that monitored their behavior through quantitative measurements.*
I have included excerpts from Mr. Garstang's book with his permission to help clarify the elephant behavior I included in my story of Baboo.
—Amy Baird

Excerpts from Professor Garstang's *Elephant Sense and Sensibility: Behavior and Cognition*

Introduction (Foreword, Ch. 1) One million years ago, elephants and their kin occupied all the continents except Australia and Antarctica. Today they are only found in Sub-Saharan Africa and parts of Asia. Elephants are intelligent, exceptionally kind, and caring of their young and each other. The cerebral cortex and the temporal lobe of the elephant's brain are the highest among mammals– even higher than in humans. The brain of an elephant calf at birth may be as high as 53% of its final size. An adult elephant is a five-ton package of possibility. Garstang demonstrates why our species needs more curiosity, caring, and understanding of the need to preserve one of the greatest gifts nature has to offer humans.

Elephant Development and Matriarchal System (Ch. 5; Ch. 9; Ch.11) Experienced elephant matriarchs carry generations of spatial knowledge that serve to preserve the herd. This knowledge is passed on by successive predecessors. This demonstrates higher rates of survivability at times of famine and drought [...] The female matriarch has such a good memory she can guide the herd to a known area with fruit trees. She can even plan out their arrival time in sync with when the fruit will ripen. A single individual, the matriarch, with clear mental attributes is elevated to a position of leadership extended over time, with no evidence of conflict or injury within the herd. Matriarchs emit a low-frequency signal when feeding and a louder lower frequency for assembling and a different call for leading the herd to water. Female elephants remain with their mother for two years and never leave the herd family during their lifetime. The daughters of the herd's matriarch often become the future matriarchs. The knowledge embedded within the matriarch's memory is transferred through shared experience of families over 40-50 years.

Male Rites of Passage (Ch.6) The males, unlike the females, must leave the herd during adolescence. In the case of elephants, the ejection of the young male at puberty not only solves problems of disruption in the herd but allows females to remain as a cohesive group while simultaneously maintaining genetic diversity and survival characteristics[...] The large, powerful, and potentially dangerous males are excluded from the group at puberty. The African Savannah bull is the heaviest among elephants and, as a matter of fact, can weigh over 14,000 pounds or 7 tons and reach a height of up to 14 feet tall.

Emotional Intelligence and Conflict Resolution (Ch. 1) Elephants are able to sense many emotions like sadness and anger. Elephants demonstrate cognitive abilities and adaptability that are remarkable. Elephant society is considered to be the most complex among all animals, except that of humans. (p. 20) Extended families form band groups, clans, and ultimately entire populations. Elephants can recognize the calls of as many as 14 other families, totalling as many as 100 other elephants [...] These calls serve to maintain the cohesion of the family group, defining the territory occupied and alerting other groups to their presence." (p. 20) This is a way they keep the peace.

Morality (Ch. 6) Elephants are among the most social animals on the planet. (Lee and Poole, 2011). Morality is intimately embedded within the raising of young and the strength of the social bonds that hold the wider family group together (de Waal, 2008); Peterson, 2011). There is a profound paradox between the drive for genetic self-advancement of the individual which is potentially at the expense and the survival of the group as a whole. In elephants, the solution seems to be in the unique matrilineal structure of their society.

Elephants as Mega-Gardeners (Ch. 3) Elephants exercise considerable control over vegetation. They keep savannahs open to grasslands and have been termed mega-gardeners (Campos-Arceiz and Blake, 2011) [...] Their droppings produce a soft, spongy surface as they walk through the forest and across the land. Savannah elephants are estimated to dispense up to 2,000 seeds per square kilometer every day (of at least 335 plant species); thereby composting and planting the earth. Some 15 tree species have been found dispersed by elephants over distances as great as 31 miles[...] Seeds dispersed by elephants germinate 57% of the time whereas only 3% of the seeds fallen under the parent tree germinate [...] The loss of animal species and, in particular, the loss of elephants could result in a radical change in the composition of the forest. The prehensile tip- like two fingers- of an elephant's trunk can pick up objects as small as a peanut and can push over a large tree and break up its branches. Using its tusk, the elephant can gouge out softer materials and form a ball to plug up a water hole for future use by the herd. The trunk can hold up to 2.5 gallons of water in its trunk.

Landmine Detection (Ch. 1) Michael Chase of Elephants Without Borders knows of the location of some 45 minefields near Angola's Luiana Partial Reserve. After the end of the civil war in Angola in 2002, many elephants were fatally injured by landmines. However, reports that within 2 years, no injuries or losses of elephants were reported. By using overlapping tracking of five GPS-collared elephants, Chase demonstrated that these elephants (both collared and herd mates) were moving through minefields without injury [...] Responding to changing circumstances (like this), elephants demonstrate remarkable cognitive abilities and adaptability. The ability to find remote locations in trackless landscapes, to deal with threats to their survival, and to formulate solutions that can be followed by the group as a whole draw upon advanced mental processes. Elephants depend on memory, making the origins of memory fundamental to elephant neural processes.

Future of Elephants (C. 14) "For a greater part of our history or about 99.9% of the time, humans and elephants have coexisted with little or no conflict… It may be just possible that with the smallest sign of tolerance exhibited by humans for the wellbeing of elephants, it will be the elephants that meet us more than halfway." If the account of elephants in this book is to have any meaning, then it calls upon our species to act with determination on behalf of our sorely tried elephant brethren. Having done so, however, the battle will not have been won. Rather, the real battle for mutual survival on this planet can then begin in earnest. Africa, despite environmental limitations… is seen by global and indigenous economists as the continent of the future. To hope that humans, in this diverse ecological continent, will be persuaded by the costly lessons we have learned to seek some equilibrium in which species other than ourselves might survive or even prosper is perhaps to hope in vain. All that has been recounted in this book, however, denies capitulation. At some point, with this and many, many more efforts, we, and elephants, as sentient beings, must prevail.

–Michael Garstang, Department of Environmental Sciences, University of Virginia, *Elephant Sense and Sensibility Behavior and Cognition* (2015)

QUESTIONS

Q: Why do you think Baboo, the young elephant, was allowed to move freely around this very special flower garden?

Q: What kind of problems did the Queen have to deal with?

Q: Why did the King say, "No one ever wins a war?"

Q: Do you think Baboo should convince Mr. Pepper to let the other animals in the kingdom visit the Queen's Flower Garden?

Q: Why is the matriarch so important to the elephant herd?

Amy Baird (Middleton) was born and raised in Portland, Oregon. She studied Child Development, Art and Architecture at Oregon State University and attended the Reed College-Portland Art Museum joint course. She earned a Bachelor of Fine Arts degree from Virginia Commonwealth University.

Her work has been influenced by the Northwest, from the rain forests of the Pacific Coast to the wild flowers in Eastern Oregon, and has been inspired by the art and cultures of Asia, Europe and the Middle East. Amy enjoys gardening and watching the many birds that drop by in the spring. She is the mother of three children and lives in the mountains of Virginia with her dog Ulla.

Other Books By Amy Baird

Blossom and Beenie
Go to Paris

By
Amy Baird

Charlie
The Brave Little Teddy Bear

Amy Baird

Someday, When I Grow Up

Amy Baird

wrensnestproductions.com

www.ingramcontent.com/pod-product-compliance
Lightning Source LLC
Chambersburg PA
CBRC090735150426
42811CB00068B/1924